The Hospital Visitor's Handbook

The Dos and Don'ts of Hospital Visitation

Neville A. Kirkwood

morehouse

HARRISBURG • LONDON

Morehouse Publishing, P.O. Box 1321, Harrisburg, PA 17105
Morehouse Publishing, The Tower Building, 11 York Road,
London SE1 7NX
Morehouse Publishing is a Continuum imprint.

Cover design by Dana Jackson

Library of Congress Cataloging-in-Publication Data

Kirkwood, Neville A.
    The hospital visitor's handbook : the dos and don'ts of hospital visitation / Neville A. Kirkwood.
        p.   cm.
    Includes bibliographical references.
    ISBN 0-8192-2200-3 (pbk.)
    1. Hospital patients—Pastoral counseling of.   2. Church work with the sick.   3. Pastoral medicine. I. Title.
BV4335.K566 2005
259'.411—dc22

                                                                2004027343

Printed in the United States of America

01 02 03 04 05 06 07 08 09   10 9 8 7 6 5 4 3 2 1

✦ CONTENTS ✦

✦ INTRODUCTION ✦

The unidentified hospital visitor comes to the hospital like any other visitor. The normal visiting hours are observed. The hospital visitor, like a pastoral visitor, is not permitted to visit people of other denominations or religions without the permission of the patient or their relatives. Where an adequate hospital security system operates, the ward staff may summon the security guard to escort the offending hospital visitor off the premises if he/she presses beyond those boundaries.

There are some hospital visitors who feel they have the right to visit every patient and leave literature with them. This breaches the Privacy Act and may offend patients who do not wish to have a religious visit.

Hospital visitors visiting a member of a local parish congregation are not obligated to report to ward staff, although that is advisable, and are generally treated like other people visiting friends or relatives. Hospital visitors are accountable to their own parish clergy.

CHAPTER 1

Off to Hospital

So you are going to visit a patient in hospital? Before you go you should know the reason that prompts you to make the decision to go. The simple question to ask before you make any move is "Why am I going?" That perhaps sounds ridiculous. It is not. The motive for your visit is a gauge against which the value of your visit will be measured. Your reason for visiting will be reflected in your attitude to the patient, and in most cases that attitude will be obvious to the patient. Too often our decision is reached without any thought of how or why the visit is being made.

Too many visitors may have an adverse effect on the progress of a patient in hospital, as well as the nature of the visit. As those who move among patients daily, chaplains and staff frequently hear expressions of relief that a visitor or visitors have at last gone. Patients are sometimes more exhausted and weak on a Monday morning after a weekend of visitors. There are also the occasions when a patient becomes very depressed following the visit of a pastoral person who speaks inappropriately.

After visits by two clergymen to different terminally ill patients, the relatives present at the time of each minister's call requested that those visitors not be allowed near the patient again. On both occasions the reading of the twenty-third Psalm, and in particular the verse that refers to the "valley of the shadow of death," caused concern and distress. In one it was the spouse who was not able to cope with the reality of the situation.

One must assume that in both cases the visitors went with the purpose of preparing the patient to face death. They had a purpose, a motive and most probably had thought out their agenda for the visit. However, it proved not only ineffective but also harmful.

WHY AM I GOING?

Questionable motives

There will be many surprises if this question is faced honestly. The reasons for hospital visitation will vary and we shall see that many are of dubious character.

Out of duty

As a relative, friend or pastoral care visitor, the reason for going to the hospital springs so often out of a sense of obligation. The fulfillment of that sense of duty hopefully will make the patient happy. Is this a trap we fall into? Are we visiting in order to be released from the guilt of unperformed responsibility? All this has a ring of selfishness about it. It is satisfying our ego. Duty can help fulfill our desire to be needed and our sense of being a martyr for the cause. It promotes the concept, which we desire other people to have of us, always being busy doing good.

Doing our job helps maintain the reputation and name we are building for ourselves. The greater the inconvenience, the greater the expected acclaim. The duty visit lacks the vital component of pastoral care: spiritual sensitivity.

The mantle's accepted

Appointed as an official hospital visitor the person assumes a certain performance framework. Lay pastoral care workers and clergy frequently fall into this trap.

A parishioner is in hospital so a visit must be made to fly the flag. In doing so, an official church visitor presumes a certain expectation by the church to perform particular functions, such as reading the Bible and praying. As I will show later, these *may* be inappropriate at that particular stage of the patient's hospitalization.

The mantle that has been assumed is likely to color the method of approaching the bedside. Naturalness and spontaneity are sometimes forsaken in order to fit the role.

Role modeling as a parish visitor often presumes that religion will be raised during the visit. Such a preconception, particularly if you know little about the patient, is as subtle as pushing a bull into a china shop to catch the attention of the proprietor.

To cheer up the patient

It must be remembered that persons under treatment in hospital are not physically well. Their whole person, body, mind and spirit in most cases, is affected by the illness or treatment. This means that they tire easily. Rest and sleep are two of the greatest components of the recuperative process.

A patient was three days out of major surgery. A good friend, a renowned pastoral visitor, came along armed with a small projector and slides of a recent holiday with the intention of providing something of interest to take the patient's mind off the pain. To entertain? To cheer up? The patient was in agony, heightened through the effort of trying to concentrate and not appear rude by nodding off for the much-needed rest. The visit lasted three hours. One wonders how many lengthy entertainment visits were made to other patients who were less understanding.

Out of curiosity or competition

Hospitals and illness hold an unusual fascination for some people. They seem to have an obsession with patients' symptoms and treatments. For this reason such people are eager to become hospital visitors.

Other folk love to know what is going on in the families of the community. The church calls for prayer for those in hospital. It is a topic for conversation. To have visited the patient in hospital is to have first-hand information and the bearer of such information becomes the center of news—that may be presented as data sincerely conveyed for the purposes of prayer. The visit and the visitor become the source for the church bulletin news flash!

Both these compulsions give rise to visits that are of little value because they are made out of curiosity, to satisfy a personal need: the need to be the center of news or attention, to be thought of as selfless and caring, to be near suffering, pain or even death, or just to be in the know as to what is going on. Such visits seldom bring support, comfort or strength to the patient.

A successful and respected pastoral carer was the envy of another person, who increased visits to a particular patient in order to outdo the first visitor. The patient knew exactly what was going on and when the jealous visitor's calls became a source of anxiety and a burden, she conveyed her feelings to the carer she valued. To spare her the strain of too many visits, and because he detested competition in Christian service, this pastoral worker cut down on his own calls. In this case, the loser was the patient.

A visit to a patient in hospital must be offered in deepest sincerity and with a genuine desire to provide positive pastoral care. Curiosity and competition are evils that have no place in the context of hospital care.

CHAPTER 2

Visiting the Patient

QUESTIONS VISITORS NEED TO ASK THEMSELVES

Does the patient need a visit?

One hospital I know has a very strict protocol concerning visitors to patients in intensive care. Only members of the immediate family and only one member of the clergy associated with the patient's church are allowed to the bedside. The chaplain of the intensive care unit has the responsibility to verify the identity of that priest, minister or rabbi. This policy had to be brought in because a patient from a family well known in religious circles had numbers of clergy popping in and causing confusion.

The wisdom of your visit at a particular time has to be considered in the light of the best interests of the patient. One patient may be too weak to see you and may need all the rest possible. Another patient may have sufficient people offering pastoral care. Remember, visitors may often unnecessarily tire and exhaust patients. At the height of the crisis you may encroach on the privacy that the family and patient require.

If your visit coincides with a patient's grief and hostility against God, your presence may increase that hostility. Your words and pious offer of prayer may do irrevocable damage, closing off all future opportunities for pastoral care. It may be the last straw that results in a total and final rejection of God. You must ask yourself seriously, "Does the patient need my visit just now or at any time?" The timing of a visit before or after surgery demands your consideration. Visits, unless there are special reasons, should be avoided until a few days after surgery. Sometimes a presurgery visit assuring prayerful support is appreciated, but at other times it may not bring any comfort. Many deeply religious and active members in the church have said that they have not told their minister or priest about hospitalization because other parishioners might then overwhelm their quiet. A private person may desire to share such an anxious time with the family only.

Would my visit be appropriate? Do your homework. Do not take it for granted.

Am I the appropriate pastoral person?

A patient had been transferred from a country hospital to the city by air ambulance. The patient's minister had contacted me, giving details of the family's journey and expected time of arrival by road. In the meantime, an aunt's city minister of another denomination appeared in the intensive care unit and gave an entirely different version of the family's movements to the nurses. That threw the staff into confusion. The fact was that the aunt's minister had it wrong. This type of situation can arise when inappropriate visits are made by pastoral visitors.

The city minister had not ascertained all the facts. While he must be commended for responding to the call, he failed to find out whether the patient had church connections, what they were, what the immediate family wished. He did not seek out the chaplains at the hospital for possible assistance, advice and information on the patient. It turned out that he was not the appropriate person to be involved at that time.

Even when someone is a member of the local

parish, she or he may not be the ideal person to provide the most significant contribution. One church elder has a real commitment to the care and support of many people both within and without the church. Her contribution is valuable as an elder. She has a strong personality, is a good organizer, and knows what a person needs. When it comes to hospital visitation, however, patients are often overwhelmed by her presence. Her kindly nature wants to mother and organize both patient and family. Sometimes that is good but not always.

Know your own strengths and weaknesses as a pastoral person. Endeavor to know and understand whether your gifts can be used with this case or whether an approach would be considered an unhelpful intrusion.

A willingness to accept that we cannot minister to all people is a major criterion for a good pastoral care person. With that principle established, it should be an automatic self-posed question: "Am I the most appropriate one to make this visit to this person or family?"

THE VISIT IS TO THE PATIENT

Having decided that you should make the visit, the next factor to concentrate upon is that the visit is *to* the patient and *for* the patient.

It is a truism that hospital patients are a captive audience. They are confined to bed. They have no means of escaping from visitors. Evangelical concern for the spiritual welfare of the patient often places expectations upon the carer to say the magical words that will produce a desired spiritual decision. This can translate into pressure on a "trapped" patient.

Every chaplain is called numerous times a year with "Will you visit Mr. X? . . . He is in your hospital seriously ill. I don't know whether he is a practicing Christian or not. Would you visit him and lead him to the Lord?"

It is such a common request. The chaplain usually replies, "I will see what the situation is and will act appropriately." More often than not, the raising of religious issues would have provoked strong negative reactions in the patient.

On one occasion I was asked to see a terminally ill retired postmaster on the terms just outlined. His two sisters were present. The whole conversation centered around his far-from-religious activities. It was one of his few lucid days. His sisters were taking advantage of it and were also receiving much comfort. It would have been most inadvisable to press eternal issues. After weeks of confusion and irrationality, he was reveling in reminiscing with his sisters. It was a memorable, comforting and happy time for all present—the last time they were to have communication with him in conversation.

Patients are very vulnerable to their spiritual needs at such times and are susceptible to any suggestions. Coercion, manipulation and, occasionally, dishonest methods are used by pastoral visitors to obtain decisions and promises about which the patient has little understanding. Often patients are in a state of mind that is not receptive to theological pronouncements on spiritual matters.

Some so-called deathbed conversions are assents to pressure tactics. Affirmations are sometimes made to relieve the pressure and make the pastoral visitor happy. Patients have admitted "anything to shut them up." That is not pastoral care. A caring relationship is not built this way. The many who have come into a deeper and closer relationship with God through the bedside ministry have usually done so after bridges have been built.

If the aim of your visit is to build a caring relationship, then your visit must be *to* and *for* the patient. You are wholly concerned with the easing of his or her burden in the Spirit of Jesus.

MAKE IT COMFORTABLE

For any relationship to be meaningful and helpful, each person must be at ease with the other.
Signs of feeling uncomfortable must be recognized immediately. If that uneasy feeling is not
dissipated, then the impossibility of a continuing
relationship should be recognized. No one person is able to be all things to all persons. To persist in the face of a continuing hostile reception
is unproductive. It can also be damaging for the
ministry of other pastoral carers who have more
in common with the person confined to bed.

There are occasions when a patient will delib-
erately make visitors feel uncomfortable in an effort to test their sincerity.

One young woman made it quite clear to me
that she didn't want to see a chaplain. A visit the
next day, in spite of the put-off, indicated my
willingness to show care and concern for this patient. The ensuing daily visits elicited her story of
a lifestyle of prostitution and many incidents in
her past At the end of her stay, with open arms
and a kiss she expressed her gratitude for my
concerned attention and sincere care, which had
weathered the test.

It took grace to go back the day after when she made it obvious that the "Not Wanted" sign had been hung out. It paid to take the rebuff on the chin and then continue to make her feel comfortable. However, if evidence of a thaw had not ensued, then it would have been a mistake to have persisted. Temper zealotry in caregiving by discerning the right moment to pull out or to continue. For care to be helpful, a sense of comfort should be tangible to all concerned.

SHOW GENUINE CONCERN

Visitors very easily fall into the trap of letting the visit become a social occasion. There are other friends also at the bedside. Some you may know from the church or other quarters. Of course, you were all at a recent church activity, that is, all except the patient. The conversation turns to that occasion and you all reminisce. You recall Mrs. X's act, you share the humor of her antics. Oh! And the outfit John Wilson wore sends you all into peals of laughter—except the patient, who has no clue of what you are all talking about. So the conversation goes on with not a word addressed to the patient except, "Oh! You should have been there." The patient is silently fuming because none of you is interested in the real purpose of your visit—to be a blessing to the one lying in the bed. The visit is marked by a lack of genuine concern.

Perhaps you have never met one of the patient's friends before. You are a keen pastoral worker. You are interested in all people. She lives in the parish area. Here is a person you may be able to get into the church's program, so you make the effort to get to know her. She used to be a physical education and aerobics teacher. You remark, "That's strange, our girls' club is looking for someone to teach aerobics. Would you be free on a Thursday night between 7 and 8?" So the conversation proceeds until you have arranged for her to see the girls' club leader and you go away feeling it was a profitable afternoon. The patient is quite depressed thinking, "The church is not really interested in me, only itself." Where was the *real* care in that visit?

All too frequently, you see visitors around a bedside with three or four conversations in progress. None is directed toward the patient, who is under tremendous strain trying to pick up the gist of each conversation. This can lead to greater and greater frustration, anxiety and a feeling of abandonment in spite of the presence of six or eight visitors. For the visitors it is a great reunion, for the ill patient, only torment and further headaches and pain.

Maybe you are the sole visitor. This is a golden opportunity for you. Instead, in the midst of your time together, your eyes wander across to another patient who is having a great time, like a king holding court with his loyal subjects. He is so amusing your eyes and ears try not to miss anything. Another patient is gasping for breath and looks very ill. The labored breathing troubles you so your concentration is on the next bed. Meanwhile your patient finds you saying "yes" and nodding when you should be saying "no." Frequently you are forced to ask that a sentence be repeated. Your eyes are not on the patient but elsewhere. The real sphere of your interest and concern is perfectly obvious to the patient. Pastoral care takes a holiday.

Why are conversations thus turned away from the patient? Often the reason is that it is easier to take in these diversions than to face the real issue of the visit, which is to offer pastoral support to a person suffering, bewildered, lonely and dependent. The patient in fact has become an embarrassment. The visitors, pastoral family and friends avoid the real issues facing this person. They shun the purpose of the visit.

We will never know how many patients feel very hurt each day, demoralized and relieved when the visitor leaves. "They were not interested in me," they say, "only themselves." The pastoral visit is *to* and *for* the patient. Keep the conscious patient the center of your attention and conversation unless he or she is so debilitated that simply having family and friends near is enough.

DEFINING PASTORAL CARE

Hospital pastoral care workers can accept the definition of pastoral care given by Hulme:

"Pastoral care is a supportive ministry to people and those close to them who are experiencing the familiar trials that characterize life in this world, such as illness, surgery, incapacitation, death and bereavement."[1]

You are therefore to support the person experiencing the necessity to be hospitalized. Alastair Campbell[2] introduces another term into such care: "pastoral relationship." This, he considers,

---

1. William E. Hulme, *Pastoral Care and Counseling Using the Unique Resources of Christian Tradition*, (Minneapolis: Augsburg, 1981), 4–13.

2. Alastair V. Campbell, *Rediscovering Pastoral Care*, (London: Darton, Longman and Todd, 1981), 10.

is the key by which we enter the world of the person. Christians care because of their own relationship with God and they are able to bring an extra dimension to the bedside. Any pastoral care offered to the hospital patient involves entering into a concerned, caring relationship with that needy patient on the part of one who is effectively motivated by a pastoral relationship with God in Christ.

In genuine pastoral care the person visited becomes aware of this other dimension in the person of the visitor. At the time the patient may not identify that difference. However, it eventually will be acknowledged as God in Christ being present in the carer. That added presence gives the patient and the relatives a calmness and increased confidence of being cared for and valued as persons.

A pastoral visit that is properly patient-centered leaves peace and assurance in its wake due to the divine presence, expressed through the visitor.

CHAPTER 3

Respecting the Patient

Visiting the hospital patient often reveals more about you than you may realize. It indicates your thoughtfulness or thoughtlessness. It shows the depth of your care. It displays the magnitude of your sincerity and genuine interest. More importantly, it broadcasts the depth of your understanding of the feelings and emotions of one confined.

FEELINGS AND EMOTIONS

A hospital ward is packed with the widest possible range of feelings and emotions. Do you readily recognize them?

Exposed

Most people have their own domain where they are able to make their own decisions and do their own thing—how, when and where they choose. Others have greater responsibility of leadership and authority from the workplace, to school, home, church or area of recreation. All of us guard jealously our privacy and rights to privacy as individuals. In ordinary life we do not like being put down, mocked or being made to look like a fool. Our mistakes, if held up to public view, cause us embarrassment. Whenever we are embarrassed, it is a blow to our dignity. Our sense of personal dignity is the measure of our self-esteem.

In hospital a patient loses many of these cherished rights. Autonomy is gone. The freedom to decide when to get up, dress, or take a shower is stripped away. For many, the ability to perform natural functions depends upon when a nurse is able to bring a pan or a bottle. The executive streak in all of us is effectively blocked for the duration of the hospital stay. Doctors, nurses and therapists make the decisions. The patient becomes the subservient one who must obey or risk deterioration of health and sometimes the effectiveness of treatment.

The curtains are pulled, the consultant, registrar, the resident, perhaps a student and a nurse gather around the bed as the patient lies bare while a thorough examination is undertaken. The patient's own feelings to such exposure are secondary to the necessity for the examination. When medical or nursing students also are present, those dozen or so pairs of eyes on you seem to pierce every part of your torso. It feels as though every mole is being counted and every private organ is being charted for shape and size. There is nothing that is sacred to the person of the patient, who feels like screaming "Exposed! Exposed!" Self-respect is often in tatters. Dignity has been stripped. The shameless cloud of inhumanity seems to be overshadowing this victim of the institution.

Useless

The man who controls a professional office, now publicly exposed at midday in his pajamas without the phone ringing to seek his direction and decisions, feels emasculated. His self-image of always being in command and productive is destroyed. In the hospital his cherished work ethic lies in tatters. This applies equally to the union organizer who expects his word to be followed without question; the bricklayer who takes pride in the straightness and neatness of his walls; or the apprentice bent on accurately reassembling the motor he has stripped.

For the principal of a renowned high school, taking orders from nurses only a few years older than her students challenges her authoritarian role. Her controlling personality and sense of dress appropriate for her status in the eyes of her pupils abandon her, as a hospital gown reduces her to equal status with the other patients. Unable to complete the reports for her administration board, the enforced idleness torments her.

The mother who bears the anxieties of a family's welfare struggles against the separation caused by hospitalization. All the mending and ironing that is mounting up because she cannot do it weighs heavily on her mind.

The popular lass who works in a government department finds no rewards in the hospital for time spent on a perfect make-up job. Her delicate nighties are not the type usually worn in a hospital. She cannot look her feminine best. She cannot do the things she normally does.

Many patients are bogged down in the despair of uselessness. Idleness does not lie easily with most people. Each hour seems to drag.

The patient you are about to visit may feel worthless. Life in hospital holds few achievement challenges.

Patients are conscious of having had taken from them that precious gift of a democratic society's independence to do and to be. This adds to the bodily "insult," which resulted in the admission to the hospital in the first place.

A burden

Independence can militate against recovery. An independent person finds it difficult to accept any help or care from others. As the word suggests, an independent person detests being dependent upon anyone. For these people, dependence implies a necessary obligation. Even though they may be paying full hospital rates through a medical insurance fund, they still feel an obligation to those providing healthcare. They develop a misguided awareness that they are a burden to society. Their occupation of the bed is precluding someone else, who may be sicker, from receiving treatment. The reasons mount as they try to find ways to prove that they are an encumbrance to others.

This feeling in some respects has the effect of firing scattershot into an empty sky: it does not target any particular person or thing. However, when the sense of being a burden to family members is voiced, complications in relationships are possible. One patient had exhausted all possible treatment for cancer and was told it was a matter of weeks. He began talking about nursing homes.

His independent nature assumed that he would be too much of a burden on his wife, that she would not be able to cope. I noticed her hurt expression as she repeated to her son, "He says that I would not be able to manage him at home." His condition had so deteriorated by the next morning that it was impossible to take the matter up with him. Was it a sense of obligation or the guilt of being a burden that he shrank from? In any case it denied the wife the privilege of caring for the one she loved, even for a few days, before he died.

This phobia of being a burden does affect the patient's ability to be able to relate to loved ones, friends and others who want to devote themselves to caring. To repeatedly have had your efforts spurned makes natural grieving following the death more difficult. Unrectifiable hurt, even when mingled with forgiveness, remains unpalatable for a long time.

Threatened

From earliest days, our culture has conditioned us to associate hospitals with death. This association stems from the days of limited medical knowledge during which many people admitted to hospital died. Presently, hospitals cure and successfully handle many illnesses. The risk of death associated with surgical procedures has been reduced dramatically. A longer life span is now possible for some cancer patients through medical treatment. Yet, the old fears still persist. There is still a majority of people who on being hospitalized see their existence threatened.

Life is the one thing on earth that has no price about it. Life is a precious commodity to be cherished and maintained at whatever cost, sometimes at the expense of quality of life. Hospitalization poses a threat to a patient's continuing to live a normal life. It shouts "change."

In a normal society any suggestion of a change stirs a certain amount of resentment. Church services can be cited as an example. The adverse response to any move for change hinges upon an ignorance of conditions that are likely after the innovation. When life is threatened, a fear of the unknown beyond death becomes mind-absorbing. Most people in the Western world have few ideas of what any future life will be like.

An eighteen-year-old remarked, after being told he had less than a week to live, "I'm not afraid of dying, only afraid of being nothing when I die." According to Christian belief, he was well astray. Yet many practicing Christians find it difficult to cope with the thought of their own death, simply because they do not know what lies on the other side.

Any threat to life raises all the fears of the unknown, of separation, of loss of mobility, independence, and friends; of pain, mutilation, unfinished business; fears for the welfare of loved ones; fears of being unable to cope with the illness, of being unable to express feelings and love; of suffering the side-effects of the treatment, and so on. We shall look at these fears in detail later.

Your visit may be to a bedside where a combination of these fears is raging in the patient's mind. Consider your sensitivity to such mental torment so as not to add to it inadvertently.

WHAT THE PATIENT NEEDS

Any of these anxieties can lead the patient into varying depths of depression. He or she has three basic needs: to be restored to health, to feel cared for and to be reassured. Hospital visitors may be able to assist in meeting some of these needs although they may be limited by the nature of the patient's mental health, the trust relationship between the visitor and the patient, lack of medical knowledge of the case or inappropriateness of the time for developing the issue.

RESTORATION OF SELF-RESPECT

Where the self-image of patients has been shattered, they require a vision of themselves as having worth in spite of their illness or threatened death. Recalling the many positive, happy and helpful things that have characterized their lives deflects the mind from the present hurt. Helping patients to recount family experiences, holidays, business or spiritual highlights begins to brighten the picture and reaffirm them as persons.

TO BE REASSURED

Reassurance can be given in many ways. There is the reassurance, for instance, that the patient is not forgotten but remembered, prayed for and respected by many others. To name names of those who enquired after them, or those who are praying for them lifts their spirits.

Where there are doubts about treatment and its effects, it is often not possible for the visitor to personally make any medical contribution. However, he or she may leave word with ward staff that the patient wants further explanation. Remember that the patient often exercises "selective hearing" for coping. That means that although the medical personnel may have repeatedly explained clinical conditions and prognosis the patient's coping ability did not permit absorption of such information. Some call this a form of denial. Often the fact is that the patient is so overwhelmed by what is happening that he or she cannot comprehend the implications of what is being said. The benefits of treatment need to be emphasized or, if no treatment is possible, then, the sick person needs to hear that adequate pain control is possible and will be given. With current palliative care programs, pain can be minimized and well controlled.

There are times when confidence in the staff and the specialist is low. The boosting of such confidence often turns an unhealthy passive attitude to the treatment into positive, optimistic co-operation with the doctors. Because of the deflation of personal ego as a result of the diagnosis and treatment, the patient may express stored-up anger at anything that can be conveniently blamed for unnecessary pain. After allowing for some ventilation of these feelings, strongly reassure the patient that there are good grounds for anticipating the best care possible.

At such crisis times people imagine God has abandoned them. To demonstrate, in the manner of Jesus, that God still cares raises the person's spirits immeasurably. The "Jesus manner" is seen in his dealings with Zaccheus, the woman at the well in Samaria, and blind Bartimaeus or in parables such as the prodigal son or the good Samaritan. An understanding, gentle approach to fostering an awareness of our loving, caring God can bring the reassurance the patient needs.

WHAT THE HOSPITAL VISITOR CAN DO

Accept patients as they are

If there is one way in which patients can feel the genuineness of care, it is when they are accepted as they are, sick, wan, depressed, irritable, exhausted, unsociable, unloving and difficult to love.

Respect patients in your own conversation

A patient doesn't want to hear *your* gripes. To talk or gossip about another person or mutual acquaintance further depresses. In any conversation with the patient a positive approach should be presented without stretching reality.

Relating your experience with your own operation or about someone else who died from the same complaint will bring an antagonistic response. Your subsequent visits will not be welcome.

One hospital visitor reveled in the opportunity to talk about the number of times she had faced death's door with a clot in the lungs. While she was able to say, "Look I'm alive," it proved to be very alarming for patients threatened with that condition. It was not appreciated particularly by one young mother with five children, who thought of the ramifications if she should die.

Watch your dress

In modern times formality of dress is very optional. Patients are sick, however, and respect shown to them is reflected in the style of your attire. A person in evening finery, "showing off" like a parading model in full array, may further crush the patient's spirit. The invalid situation is rubbed in. On the other hand, dirty jeans, revealing tops and thongs shout disrespect for the patient: "I'm not worth much, look how they dress."

Dress moderately, cleanly, tidily and in keeping with your role as a person visiting a hospital patient The staff also will pay you the respect you deserve as evidenced by your manner of dress.

Don't do the things that patients can do for themselves

When patients have dropped their bundle, and defeat stares them in the face, they need to be encouraged to do things for themselves, such as simply pouring a glass of water. Don't emphasize their weaknesses, incapacity or invalidism by being too helpful. The sense of achievement gained by doing something for themselves is great therapy.

Where the condition is terminal, causing business or personal accomplishments to be restrained or even abandoned, the question is often asked, "What have I done to deserve this?" Drawing attention to those achievements and days of happiness helps lift the vision from the depression and enables her or him to see that the question is irrelevant to the situation.

A patient may sink lower into depression if there is a trace of dishonesty or patronizing insincerity in efforts to restore self-respect. Genuineness and honesty must characterize any relationship and conversation. To be patronizing or condescending destroys even further the patient's self-esteem.

To feel cared for

This is where a visit out of a sense of duty or responsibility is detected. Your visit should be made out of deep concern for the patient. The one on the bed needs tender loving care, not the breezy "I'm here to see you, buck up and get on with the job, get better, let's read a prayer and I'll be off" attitude. When the patient is exhausted, in pain or just confused as to what is happening, a truly gentle approach is necessary:

"I see you are weary and just want to sleep and rest. I've come to let you know I really care and am praying for you. I'll continue to do it. You just get as much rest as possible and I'll come back when you are not so exhausted."

A visit of such short time and few words may be one of the most valuable visits ever made to a hospital patient. Conversely, much time and many words may only show just how insensitive a visitor is to the patient's condition and need.

The hospital visitor is able to do much to bring encouragement and support into the lives of the ailing, and recognition of their personal value.

✣ CHAPTER 4 ✦

Observe

You have thought about the motive for the hospital visit and are convinced that you should make the call. You understand a little of what the patient's attitude to his or her illness may be and what he or she may need from you. The next question is "What more can I do?" The first essential of any approach to patients is the ability to observe all you can as you enter the hospital and the ward.

THOSE HOSPITAL SIGNS

Look for hospital notices. The first signs the visitor should heed are the ones relating to traffic. One-way and parking signs, like all laws and regulations, have been installed out of experience and necessity.

Being in a hurry and having an exaggerated view of the importance of the visitor's role can lead to the temptation to park in a disabled drivers' zone. Or a space in a fifteen-minute parking spot is looked on as convenient and time-saving. Parking close to the hospital is often considered an essential prerequisite by visitors. Sometimes the accident and emergency parking areas have empty spaces that are appropriated on the grounds, "I'm a hospital visitor doing my good deed. I'm doing this voluntarily, therefore the authorities won't object. They will understand."

It is very convenient to rationalize our action of parking illegally but would we take such liberties with signs outside the police station? Signs outside the hospital building are placed there for the ease and welfare of our fellow human beings, as are the signs inside.

Most hospitals have clearly marked notices on every floor as to the visiting hours, and some hospitals are more strict with such hours than others. Whether the policy is rigid or lenient for the hospital visitor, it is courtesy to respect it. The patient's own parish minister or priest may be exceptions to the visiting hours rules, but generally speaking, these privileges should not be misused or abused.

Visiting hours are recommended for the good of the patients. In the average hospital patients find it difficult to get a good night's sleep and some use sleeping tablets, only to find that the sedation and dopiness can take most of the morning to wear off. When this is the case, the struggle to keep awake for the hospital visitor adds stress, anxiety, embarrassment and further exhaustion. The arrival of visitors outside the approved hours often finds the patient too tired to appreciate the visit.

Nonvisiting hours are generally in the morning when doctors are involved in rounds or when treatment, tests and dressings are attended to. Pastoral visiting at these times may be interrupted by medical personnel so that meaningful involvement with the patient is not possible.

Other signs such as "Restricted Visiting," "Please See Nursing Unit Manager" or "No Visitors" are for the protection of the patient whose condition may be such that there is a risk of visitors increasing harmful stress when rest is interrupted. In some cases the patient may not want to see certain visitors and requests a monitoring of callers. If you are an official church hospital visitor, it is appropriate to see the nursing unit manager to introduce yourself and confirm the convenience of your visit.

"Isolation" may be the word that is prominent at the patient's door. This particular sign is in place for two reasons. Firstly the patient may have an infectious disease, so the visitor needs protection. In the second case, the patient's immune system may be so low that he or she runs the risk of being infected by any germ or virus the visitor may introduce into the ward. Such infection could develop into a major setback.

"Nil by mouth" (NPO) and "restricted fluids" are warnings or instructions for patients, staff and visitors. Prior to surgery, an empty stomach is essential. Even a sip of water may have its effect upon the patient either in theater or after the operation. Or the patient's kidneys may not be able to rid the body of excess fluid; hence the need to be on a severely controlled fluid intake. (Often the fluid intake is measured against the output to keep a check on the effectiveness of the drug dosage or kidney function.) It has been known for the unwary visitor to be conned into relieving the poor thirsty sufferer without the nurse knowing. I recall a case where the visitor was asked to help clean the patient's teeth, and then the patient gulped down all the rinsing water.

If staff cooperation is expected, or your role as a pastoral visitor is to be accepted in the ward, then obviously signs must be heeded.

OBSERVE THE PATIENT

Your observation of the patient is critical to the success of your visit. A correct assessment of the patient's condition and mood permit you to make the most appropriate introduction.

Looks provide the key to condition. Is the patient wan, listless, sleepy, or alert and smiling? Depressed or pleased to see you? Indifferent to your presence or teary, flushed, breathless? Worse or improved since your last visit? The "hail-fellow-well-met" approach to a depressed or extremely weak patient brings an unverbalized reaction of "get out of here." Such a visit will be considered as insensitive and insincere. Similarly patients struggling and slowly making improvement are not impressed by being told they look dreadful. This may break their spirit, particularly if they were just starting to feel a bit better. To the same patient equally inappropriate are words such as "you're looking splendid."

Your observation of the patient's physical condition will give you clear leads as to how your meeting will develop. One important decision that should be a result of your assessment by observation is the length of time you should stay (see supplements 1 and 2).

Patient showing weakness

This calls for a short visit with few words. Concentration on conversation may load further strain and stress onto the patient, which can accelerate fatigue and debilitation.

Patient looking depressed

The need may be for a quick hello and goodbye or even a long, silent time of just holding hands and an effort to assess the reasons for the despondency. The assessment may have to be reappraised as the visit develops or on subsequent visits.

Patient showing signs of pain

Seriously ill patients, both medical and surgical, may experience much bodily discomfort and pain. Their condition can be so agonizing that they are on painkillers such as pethidine (demerol) or morphine, and they may be unable to cope with much beyond their own concerns. Their concentration span is extremely short. In fact the need to concentrate on anything but their condition is distressing, and the discomfort is aggravated by a hospital visitor coming in with a smiling face and words such as, "Well, the Lord knows and understands your condition. Leave it in his hands and just trust." At this point, patients could feel like screaming but have to bottle up the anger, which only increases the pain and trauma.

Patient's reaction to the visit

The patient's first sighting of you frequently produces facial expressions or bodily movements which indicate that your visit is welcome or otherwise. Be sensitive to that initial reaction. Those indicators should determine the length of your stay. One day the patient may not be up to a visit. The next day or next week it may be different. Hostility toward God, with its recoil back onto anyone from the church, needs to be considered as a possible reaction. It is unwise to take the attitude, "They are angry. I must reconcile them with God. This is my mission." You will only drive in the wedge further against God.

A good look at the patient should reveal much concerning what you should do. To think that you have the answer for him or her and that this is your mission may be out of touch with God's plans for ministry to that patient at that time. Your need to help people should not get in the way of correctly observing the patient.

OBSERVE THE WARD

Whether you are meeting the ailing for the first time or are well acquainted, the perusal of the ward is likely to provide indicators of what's happening for the patient. A bare table and a shelf with no flowers or cards may point to a lonely person requiring lots of attention. It may also declare that this well-known person has not publicized the hospitalization to church or friends and is seeking quiet. Except where there are clear contrary markers, the visitor should not be presumptive and outstay the welcome or tell others that the patient is in hospital. The patient's right to confidentiality and privacy must be respected.

Lots of cards and flowers shout out for all to see: this patient is loved and well cared for. It is possible that your attention to him or her is not as necessary as to some other sick folk. On the other hand, that show of popularity may indicate that the person is a great game player, a very gregarious, life-of-the-party person, whom no one really knows. Perhaps nobody can get very close. Hospitalization may be the one opportunity for a skillful hospital visitor to ease the clam open and discover the real person. Such revelation, if handled rightly, may be an instrument leading to real growth and development for the patient. However, it is unwise to start something you can't handle. With permission, refer to someone else.

More frequently the multitude of cards and flowers do tell what kind of support patients have. Religious cards possibly indicate good prayer support. Cards and flowers provide the opportunity for the patient to share something of themselves, their family and friends. Flowers not from the florist may indicate the patient's own love of gardening or a spouse's keen gardening pursuits. The degree of companionship in the marriage may show through.

A handmade card by an offspring or grandchild may provide some family background upon which the relationship with the visitor is developed. An expensive card may become a focal point of the conversation, with the sender described as a significant person in the patient's life, who provided support at a point of earlier crisis. The telling of that crisis episode may trigger current feelings, attitudes and relationship issues that can be poignant matters. Here the visitor's ministry may make a vital contribution.

Photographs of either family or friends are sometimes on the bedside table. These can tell stories and give indications of the family dynamics. If there is sufficient trust, these are often shared.

Observation of the ward when it is a multiple-bed one may reveal an intensely depressing spectacle. The nature of the surgery, the degree of the illness of the patient, the noise of other patients' relatives and friends, the groans and moans of another, or the lonely patient who wants to be part of your conversation, perhaps listening to all you say—all this often strains your patient's patience. Your adeptness in allowing a ventilation of these feelings may prove to be of invaluable assistance.

The perceptiveness of the pastoral caller in the initial minutes of the visit is a crucial factor in hospital visitation.

The effectiveness of any relational development depends upon the patient's ability to detect in you genuine care and not merely the spirit of the "do-gooder." The visiting person has to earn acceptance and trust. Often that right is gained through those early moments of observation. Where adequate care is being offered, be Christian enough to bow out without feeling hurt, letting others do the job. You may not be God's choice for this particular person. Care where God wants you to care.

OBSERVE THE UNSPOKEN

Vulnerable, helpless, dependent feelings often overwhelm patients. They want to give the impression of coping and not needing the sympathy being offered. Accepting sympathy or pity is a demoralizing experience. Illness seriously dents the pride and ego of many independent folk who are now confined, restricted and incapacitated. In order to avoid further self-conscious humiliation, masks are put on to distract the visitor from their real suffering.

The feeling of the injustice of the illness promotes anger. That anger is often turned Godward. "Why me?" "I've done nothing to deserve this." "I've been faithful in my church activities." These may be expressed openly or otherwise. When verbalized, the sentiment may be uttered in a placid, accepting tone. The stoic sufferer is the front put forward by many, including those renowned for their self-control, initiative, drive, coping ability and leadership skills. It is important to them that the public image be maintained.

Detection of such stoicism is important. It may be possible for you to delicately let your suspicions be known. This may allow a degree of self-disclosure. Lack of subtlety may force up irremovable barriers, so caution is needed in handling such cases. The observant visitor is alert and able to detect whether the words coming from the mouth match the communication from body and facial movements. The unspoken may be evident in the way the patient parries questions on certain subjects, deflecting the conversation into another direction. Those thrusts that come too near to the core of the truth are threatening, causing observable protective measures to be taken.

On some occasions, when there has been a good rapport established with the patient, it may be appropriate to face the issue head-on. However, seldom does such a confrontation prove profitable on an initial visit. Rather, it tends to put up shutters that remain closed to the visitor. Tuck the observation into the mind's computer, to be recalled and developed at the appropriate time.

If the temptation to rush in too soon is not resisted, there is a greater need to observe the more pronounced positive and negative vibes issuing from the patient. If they are negative here is a second chance to avoid a fouling of the lines of communication. Accept this second opportunity to act aright. In my experience patients have often complained that they have been forced too soon to face issues for which they were not ready. There is a tendency for social workers and others to prematurely open up the subject of death and dying. Pastoral visitors must be observant enough not to do the same.

Nor should they prematurely raise the issue of the patient's preparedness for the future life while the negative, disinterested or denial signs are being flashed. The visitor must be courteous enough to respect and react appropriately to these unspoken warnings. In many cases they would be wiser to leave such issues to trained pastoral care workers.

→ CHAPTER 5 ←

Relatives and Friends

The nature of the illness and the condition of the patient elicit a range of emotions and responses. The patient is not the only one experiencing such reactions of heart and spirit. Relatives, friends and even staff become involved in emotional expressions—from elation over a healthy birth to grim forebodings at the bedside of an intensive care patient comatose from septicemia.

At this point it is wise for us to recognize that these people also require pastoral care. As a hospital visitor, it may be your privilege to provide a supportive, understanding, caring touch to others as well as the patient. In fact, your nurturing of relatives or friends may be of real value to the patients, who sense that their loved ones are responding with less agitation, more confidence and less self-pity.

That supportiveness is best recognized and appreciated when you share their feelings of gladness or sadness. The ability to enter into the feelings of others is termed *empathy*. Empathy stands distinctly apart from sympathy. A patient's perception of true empathy is usually extremely acute when very ill and even sometimes when heavily medicated. In a comatose state, hearing is still possible and the patient can record in the subconscious what was said by those at the bedside.

When anguish or depression is deep, it may be beyond the limits of your expertise or training. Do refer such cases to a better-equipped pastoral person. It may not necessarily be your minister or priest.

When the patient's condition is serious, the various family members display some of the typical dynamics of grief, such as fear, guilt, anger, bewilderment, denial, depression, frustration and withdrawal. It is good therapy to allow them to verbalize or even physically express their grief. In encouraging such behavior, the visitor should not be trapped into overinvolvement with the anger, guilt etc. It is our responsibility to maintain a position from which we, at all times, are able to view the situation objectively.

Take, for instance, a case where a man had been involved in an industrial accident. The hand had been crushed. The forearm had been severely lacerated, with ligament and muscle damage. The doctor provided the relatives with a straightforward description of the nature of the wounds, and told them that Tony was going to have surgery to remove the four fingers and part of the palm. Every effort would be made to save the thumb. It depended upon what was discovered in the operating room as to exactly what would be done. The consent form for the operation was signed by Tony's father.

During surgery it was revealed that there was greater damage to the wrist bones than the x-ray had showed. Also, the ligament, muscle and nerve damage was more extensive than had been observable in Accident and Emergency. Reluctantly they had to amputate the hand just above the wrist.

On hearing this news, Tony's father, mother and one brother started screaming abuse at all who came near. "Incompetent doctors! They fouled things up! Through negligence he has lost his whole hand! We will sue the doctors!" and so on. A hospital visitor could have been manipulated into taking Tony's parents' side. They sounded so convincing. The atmosphere was emotionally charged. The empathy would have become unsoundly based on a one-sided version of events.

A visitor can no longer provide real care for a family if he or she is being controlled. The perspective would be lost. The staff might also lose respect for the visitor because of the unreasoned stance being taken. Listen, support and care without becoming the family's crusader when the ground is thin. Refrain from adding fuel to a futile fire. Keep your lips sealed, free from taking sides, until the facts are confirmed from other information.

In each family, the closeness and depth of relationship varies from person to person. The nature of these relationships needs to be understood during a traumatic hospitalization. One family member may be talkative; another moves away in withdrawn silence; others just weep and cling to each other; there may be the defiant one or two with a chip on the shoulder concerning the patient or other family members present. In some cases, they may snap at one another, trying to apportion blame. It is unwise of course to get into family feuds. Perhaps the self-isolationist needs a silent arm about them, away from the others. Oftentimes in such circumstances, a nonverbal presence is all that is necessary. The twin ministries of presence and touch convey the concern of the God we represent under these circumstances.

Unless you are well skilled in ministering to the grieving, the fewer words said the better. Along with this, the acumen to discern whether or not you are treading on private ground needs to be sharpened. If you stay around when you are not appreciated, it makes the grieving harder and aggravates the already-sensitive, angry emotions. There may be family friends who are more acceptable to the family at the time of your visit. Acknowledge it to yourself. Excuse yourself, assuring the family of your continued interest in them.

Family relationships are intricate and, as I have already said, vary from family to family and between members of the same family. It is unwise to take any family situation for granted. Some family members may be active churchgoers, others may be far from sympathetic to the church. The ability of pastoral people to maintain the confidence of all family factions requires perception as well as divine wisdom. If both are liberally exercised, a valuable healing and unifying ministry is possible. The bedside provides opportunities for reconciliation between family members, and family members and God. An acceptable, sensitive hospital visitor or other pastoral person may be the catalyst for such reconciliations.

Ministry to the family should be treated with awe. It is a task filled with responsibility. There may be resentment, feelings of intrusion, accents of guilt, or the warmth of glad acceptance. With the concurrence of the family, the hospital visitor, with the genuineness of true pastoral care may be able to generate a harmony and strength previously lacking.

During times of distress the visitor will be privy to some very personal matters and understanding of family dynamics. In times of crisis, the pastoral carer becomes like an unofficial adopted family member. Intentionally, I am repetitious here. Whatever you hear at the bedside or with the family, consider it as privileged confidential knowledge.

Healthy family and social relations are important at any stage of hospitalization. Whatever a hospital visitor or other pastoral person does to maintain and encourage such family solidarity is a major contribution to pastoral care.

It cannot be stressed too much that those who make hospital visits in the name of the church should avail themselves of every opportunity to participate in pastoral care training programs. Appropriate seminars or workshops are very helpful in forming more effective visitors/carers. If your church does not have regular pastoral care training sessions, enquire what can be done to fill the need. If you intend to be a regular hospital visitor, who has an acceptable ministry, equipping yourself for the task is essential.

Nonverbal Communication Indicators

In many cases communication between individuals involves words that carry less influence than bodily movements and expressions. Nonverbal signals, as they are called, are communicated by each person in any encounter. In visiting the hospital patient, irrespective of role, the visitor needs to observe these telltale pointers to understand the real message that patient, relative or staff is really sending. Outlined here are some of these message-carrying signs that you should observe at the bedside.

Both during and after visits, try to recall those indicators. Remember that *you also* relay messages with your own voice and body. At the time of each visit, be aware of the countermessages you may be signaling. Assess how you think the patient is reading you.

Facial expressions and appearance

POSITIVE	NEGATIVE
Warm, inviting, smiling	Cold, stiff, distant
Appropriate dress	Too formal, too casual dress
Groomed appearance (hair, make-up)	Careless appearance
Good eye contact	Roving or staring eyes, or no direct contact

Voice modulation

POSITIVE	NEGATIVE
Warm, natural	Dull, monotone
Circumspect tone	Embarrassingly loud or too soft
Understandable rate of speech	Too fast or too clipped speech
Fluent language	Stuck for words
Empathetic (understanding, supporting tone)	Artificial, false, insincere
Audible responses (*hm, hmm, aha,* etc;)	Hesitant, with many *ers, ums* and *ahs*
Appropriate silent gaps (for reflection)	Embarrassed silence with fidgeting
Interrupting to clarify or reflect before proceeding	Saying "yes, yes" when it should be "no"

Body posture

POSITIVE	NEGATIVE
Leaning toward person at eye level	Sitting side on (discouraging to relationship and interaction)
Comfortable and relaxed position, settled, making it obvious that time is no problem	Cold, rigid, impersonal attitude; remaining standing an authoritative in position; looking ready to leave momentarily
Where possible, being three to four feet distant	Too distant or too close

Gestures and manners

POSITIVE	NEGATIVE
Extended, accepting arm/s	Arms by the side, in an indifferent manner
Firm handshake if appropriate	Limp handshake
Keeping head and body turned toward patient to indicate full attention; making patient the center of conversation	Talking to others, ignoring patient, yawning, fidgeting with anything, looking frequentlyat clock or watch

Voice Characteristics and Their Meaning

Your tone of voice and the tempo of your speaking often indicate sincerity or lack of sincerity behind the words you utter. Become alert to these factors in your own bedside visits. Your hospital awareness may be sharpened by observing voice characteristics in television programs.

Voice characteristics and their meaning

Monotone	Boredom
Slow speed, low pitch	Depression
High voice, empathetic speed	Enthusiasm
Ascending tone	Astonishment
Terse speech and loud tone	Anger
High pitched, drawn-out speech	Disbelief
Short guttural sounds	Impatience

→ SUPPLEMENT 3 ←

Death and You

1. How many deceased persons have you seen? Have you been present when somebody drew their last breath? Recall your feelings at the time.
2. Describe your last encounter with a dying person or a person who nearly died. What anxieties were raised in you? Are you more or less confident about sitting with a dying patient now?
3. What do you understand when Paul calls death an enemy? Do you see death as an enemy? How does your answer to question 2 affect your attitude to a dying person?
4. Kubler-Ross entitled a book *Death: The Final Stage of Growth.* Does such a concept help you in your ideas about death?

59

5. Have you thought about your own death? Are you frightened, anxious, very anxious, apprehensive or accepting of thoughts about your own death?

6. How would you feel if you were told you had one hour to live? Are you prepared for your own death?

Your serious consideration of these points will identify your suitability to minister to terminally ill or dying patients and their relatives.

Allow sufficient time to work through each question. Write down your thoughts and share them with another pastoral care person or an active Christian, who is experienced in bereavement counseling or in the care of the dying in hospital.